architecture without architects

architecture without architects

A Short Introduction to Non-Pedigreed Architecture

by Bernard Rudofsky

Doubleday & Company, Inc., Garden City, New York

Architecture Without Architects was originally published by the Museum of Modern Art, New York

ISBN: 0-385-07487-5
© 1964, Bernard Rudofsky
Designed by Bernard Rudofsky
Printed in the U.S.A.
15   14   13   12

Acknowledgements

The exhibition *Architecture Without Architects,* shown at the Museum of Modern Art from November 9, 1964 to February 7, 1965, was commissioned by the Department of Circulating Exhibitions under the auspices of the International Council of the Museum of Modern Art. Both the exhibition and the accompanying publication were prepared and designed by the author, Consultant to the Department of Architecture and Design.

The John Simon Guggenheim Memorial Foundation and the Ford Foundation helped to finance the research for this project by awarding fellowships to the director of the exhibition for a study of non-formal, non-classified architecture. These grants might never have been given without the enthusiastic recommendations of the architects Walter Gropius, Pietro Belluschi, José Luis Sert, Richard Neutra, Gio Ponti, Kenzo Tange, and the Museum's Director, René d'Harnoncourt, all of whom hail from countries rich in vernacular architecture.

Sincere thanks go to the many people, too numerous to list here, who contributed to this project in various ways. Special tributes, however, are due to Mme. Renée Heyum, Musée de l'Homme, Paris; Miss Ruth M. Anderson, The Hispanic Society of America, New York; the staff of the Frobenius Institute, Frankfurt, and Dr. Myron B. Smith, Islamic Archives, Washington, D.C. Research assistance was rendered with exemplary patience by Miss Ellen Marsh. Credits for photographs, many of which were generously donated, are listed on the last page.

Bernard Rudofsky

Vernacular architecture does not go through fashion cycles. It is nearly immutable, indeed, unimprovable, since it serves its purpose to perfection. As a rule, the origin of indigenous building forms and construction methods is lost in the distant past. Below, houses typical of the Mediterranean area.

1

Preface   Architectural history, as written and taught in the Western world, has never been concerned with more than a few select cultures. In terms of space it comprises but a small part of the globe—Europe, stretches of Egypt and Anatolia—or little more than was known in the second century A.D. Moreover, the evolution of architecture is usually dealt with only in its late phases. Skipping the first fifty centuries, chroniclers present us with a full-dress pageant of "formal" architecture, as arbitrary a way of introducing the art of building as, say, dating the birth of music with the advent of the symphony orchestra. Although the dismissal of the early stages can be explained, though not excused, by the scarcity of architectural monuments, the discriminative approach of the historian is mostly due to his parochialism. Besides, architectural history as we know it is equally biased on the social plane. It amounts to little more than a who's who of architects who commemorated power and wealth; an anthology of buildings of, by, and for the privileged—the houses of true and false gods, of merchant princes and princes of the blood—with never a word about the houses of lesser people. Such preoccupation with noble architecture and architectural nobility to the exclusion of all other kinds may have been understandable as late as a generation ago, when the relics and ruins of ancient buildings served the architect as his sole models of excellence (to which he helped himself as a matter of course and convenience), but today, when the copying of historical forms is on the wane, when banking houses or railroad stations do not necessarily have to resemble prayers in stone to inspire confidence, such self-imposed limitation appears absurd.

Architecture Without Architects attempts to break down our narrow concepts of the art of building by introducing the unfamiliar world of nonpedigreed architecture. It is so little known that we don't even have a name for it. For want of a generic label, we shall call it vernacular, anonymous, spontaneous, indigenous, rural, as the case may be. Unfortunately, our view of the total picture of anonymous architecture is distorted by a shortage of documents, visual and otherwise. Whereas we are reasonably well informed about the artistic objectives and technical proficiency of painters who lived 30,000 years before our time, archaeologists consider themselves lucky when they stumble over the vestiges of a town that goes back to the third millennium B.C. only. Since the question of the beginnings of architecture is not only legitimate but bears heavily on the theme of the exhibition, it is only proper to allude, even if cursorily, to possible sources.

A nation that swears by the Bible also finds it an incomparable book of reference. Alas, the explicitness of the Scriptures in matters of architecture is never as disconcerting as when we learn (Genesis IV: 17) that Adam's son Cain built a city and named it after his son Enoch. A one-family town, delightful as it sounds, is a most extravagant venture and surely was never repeated in the course of history. If it proves anything, it illustrates the breathtaking progress made within a single generation, from the blessed hummingbird existence in well-supplied Paradise to the exasperatingly complicated organism that is a town. Skeptics who dismiss Enoch as a chimera will find more significance in the Ark, particularly in view of the fact that it was commissioned by the Lord Himself and built to His specifications. The question whether the Ark ought to be called a building or a nautical craft is redundant. The Ark had no keel, the keel being an intellectual invention of later days, and we may safely assume that ships were not known as yet, since their existence would have defeated the very purpose of the Flood. When Noah landed on Mount Ararat he was 601 years old, a man past his prime. He preferred to devote the rest of his life to viniculture and left the task of building to his sons. The Bible mentions (Genesis IX: 27) Shem's huts—probably put together with some of the Ark's lumber—but the decline in architecture was sealed.

The impious who prefer to turn to science in their quest for the origins of architecture will have to swallow a few indigestible facts. For it seems that long before the first enterprising man bent some twigs into a leaky roof, many animals were already accomplished builders. It is unlikely that beavers got the idea of building dams by watching human dam-builders at work. It probably was the other way. Most likely, man got his first incentive to put up a shelter from his cousins, the anthropomorphous apes. Darwin observed that the orang in the islands of the Far East, and the chimpanzees in Africa, build platforms on which they sleep, "and, as both species follow the same habit, it might be argued that this was due to instinct, but we cannot feel sure that it is not the result of both animals having similar wants, and possessing similar powers of reasoning." Untamed apes do not share man's urge to seek shelter in a natural cave, or under an overhanging rock, but prefer an airy scaffolding of their own making. At another point in *The Descent of Man,* Darwin writes that "the orang is known to cover itself at night with the leaves of the Pandanus"; and Brehm noted that one of his baboons "used to protect itself from the heat of the sun by throwing a straw-mat over his head. In these habits," he conjectured, "we probably see the first steps towards some of the

2

North American tree dwellers. The eviction scene is from Erasmus Francisci's *Lustgarten,* 1668.

Floating Village, China. From Erasmus Francisci's *Lustgarten,* 1668.

simpler arts, such as *rude architecture* and dress, as they arise among the early progenitors of man." (Our italics.) Suburban man falling asleep near his lawn mower, pulling a section of his Sunday paper over his head, thus re-enacts the birth of architecture.

Yet even before men and beasts walked the earth, there existed some kind of architecture, coarsely modeled by the primeval forces of creation and occasionally polished by wind and water into elegant structures (fig. 19). Natural caves, especially, hold a great fascination for us. Caves, having been among man's earliest shelters, may turn out to be his last ones. At any rate, they were chosen with great foresight as depositories for our most precious artifacts—government and business files. It is of course not within the scope of this exhibition to furnish a capsule history of nonpedigreed architecture, nor even a sketchy typology. It merely should help us to free ourselves from our narrow world of official and commercial architecture.

Although exotic arts have long been appreciated in the Western world—not, however, without being cautiously dubbed "primitive"—exotic architecture (the word exotic is here used in its original meaning, alien) has evoked no response, and is still relegated to the pages of geographic and anthropological magazines. Indeed, apart from a few regional studies and scattered notes, no literature exists on the subject. Lately though, ever since the art of traveling has suffered conversion into an industry, the charms of "picture-postcard towns" and the "popular" architecture of "fairy-tale countries" have proved of considerable attraction. Still, our attitude is plainly condescending.

No doubt the picturesque element abounds in our photographs, yet, again, the exhibition is not an exercise in quaintness nor a travel guide, except in the sense that it marks a point of departure for the exploration of our architectural prejudices. It is frankly polemic, comparing as it does, if only by implication, the serenity of the architecture in so-called underdeveloped countries with the architectural blight in industrial countries. In orthodox architectural history, the emphasis is on the work of the individual architect; here the accent is on communal enterprise. Pietro Belluschi defined communal architecture as "a communal art, not produced by a few intellectuals or specialists but by the spontaneous and continuing activity of a whole people with a common heritage, acting under a community of experience." It may be argued that this art has no place in a raw civilization, but even so, the lesson to be derived from this architecture need not be completely lost to us.

There is much to learn from architecture before it became an expert's art. The untutored builders in space and time—the protagonists of this show—demonstrate an admirable talent for fitting their buildings into the natural surroundings. Instead of trying to "conquer" nature, as we do, they welcome the vagaries of climate and the challenge of topography. Whereas we find flat, featureless country most to our liking (any flaws in the terrain are easily erased by the application of a bulldozer), more sophisticated people are attracted by rugged country. In fact, they do not hesitate to seek out the most complicated configurations in the landscape. The most sanguine of them have been known to choose veritable eyries for their building sites—Machu Picchu, Monte Alban, the craggy bastions of the monks' republic on Mount Athos, to mention only some familiar ones.

The tendency to build on sites of difficult access can be traced no doubt to a desire for security but perhaps even more so to the need of defining a community's borders. In the old world, many towns are still solidly enclosed by moats, lagoons, glacis, or walls that have long lost their defensive value. Although the walls present no hurdles to invaders, they help to thwart undesirable expansion. The very word urbanity is linked to them, the Latin *urbs* meaning walled town. Hence, a town that aspires to being a work of art must be as finite as a painting, a book, or a piece of music. Innocent as we are of this sort of planned parenthood in the field of urbanistics, we exhaust ourselves in architectural proliferation. Our towns, with their air of futility, grow unchecked—an architectural eczema that defies all treatment. Ignorant as we are of the duties and privileges of people who live in older civilizations, acquiesce as we do in accepting chaos and ugliness as our foreordained fate, we neutralize any and all misgivings about the inroads of architecture on our lives with lame protests directed at nobody in particular.

Part of our troubles results from the tendency to ascribe to architects—or, for that matter, to all specialists—exceptional insight into problems of living when, in truth, most of them are concerned with problems of business and prestige. Besides, the art of living is neither taught nor encouraged in this country. We look at it as a form of debauch, little aware that its tenets are frugality, cleanliness, and a general respect for creation, not to mention Creation.

To no small degree, this situation came about through the diligence of the historian. By invariably emphasizing the parts played by architects and their patrons he has obscured the talents and achievements of the anonymous builders, men whose concepts sometimes verge on the utopian, whose esthetics approach the sublime. The beauty of this architecture has long been dismissed as accidental, but today we should be able to recognize it as the result of rare good sense in the handling of practical problems. The shapes of the houses, sometimes transmitted through a hundred generations (fig. 146), seem eternally valid, like those of their tools.

Above all, it is the *humaneness* of this architecture that ought to bring forth some response in us. For instance, it simply never occurs to us to make streets into oases rather than deserts. In countries where their function has not yet deterio-

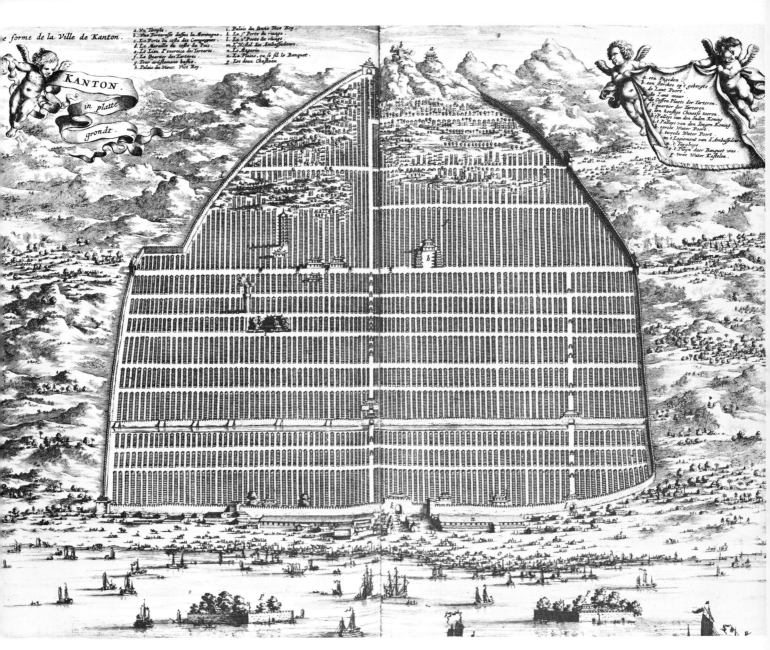

e forme de la Ville de Kanton.

a. Vn Temple.
b. Vne Forteresse dessus la Montagne.
c. La Porte du costé des Campagnes.
d. La Ruuelle du costé de l'Eau.
e. Le Lieu d'exercice des Tartare.
f. Le Quartier des Tartares.
g. Tour anciennement bastie.
h. Palais du Vieux Vice Roy.

i. Palais du Bono Vice Roy.
k. La Porte du riuage.
l. La Porte du riuage.
m. L'Hostel des Ambassadeurs.
n. Le Magasin.
o. La Plaine, ou se fit le Banquet.
p. Les deux Chasteau.

a. een Pagoden
b. een kercke op 't geberghte
de Lant Poore
meur
d. de Ceffen Plaets der Tarteren
quartier der Tarteren
een konstige Chinees tooren
h. Pallays van den Ouden Koning
i. eerste Water Poort
k. tweede Water Poort
l. Logiement van d'Ambassadeur
m. 't Tuyghuys
n. 't Pleyn daer Banquet was
p. twee Water Kastelen

KANTON. in platte grondt.

rated into highways and parking lots, a number of arrangements make streets fit for humans: pergole and awnings (that is, awnings spread across a street), tentlike structures, or permanent roofs. All are characteristic of the Orient, or countries with an oriental heritage, like Spain. The most refined street coverings, a tangible expression of civic solidarity—or, should one say, of philanthropy—are arcades. Unknown and unappreciated in our latitudes, the function of this singularly ingratiating feature goes far beyond providing shelter against the elements or protecting pedestrians from traffic hazards. Apart from lending unity to the streetscape, they often take the place of the ancient forums. Throughout Europe, North Africa, and Asia, arcades are a common sight because they also have been incorporated into

4   Town plan of Canton, China. From L'Ambassade de la Compagnie Orientale, 1665.

"formal" architecture. Bologna's streets, to cite but one example, are accompanied by nearly twenty miles of *portici*.

Another alien type of the communal vernacular is the storehouse for food. In societies where food is looked upon as a divine gift rather than an industrial product, the architecture of granaries is solemn. So much so that to the uninitiated it suggests ecclesiastical buildings. Although small in scale, storehouses achieve monumentality, whether in the Iberian peninsula, in the Sudan, or in Japan. In view of their great stylistic purity and precious content, we have termed them quasi-sacral.

Apart from the High Vernacular—the sophisticated *minor* architecture of Central Europe, the Mediterranean, South and East Asia—and primitive architecture proper, the exhibition also includes such categories as architecture by subtraction, or *sculpted* architecture, exemplified by troglodyte dwellings and free-standing buildings cut from live rock and hollowed out. Rudimentary architecture is represented by wind screens which sometimes attain gigantic dimensions. In Japan they may shield, indeed, envelop a house, a hamlet, or an entire village. Of the architecture of nomads, portable houses, houses on wheels, sled-houses, houseboats, and tents are shown. Proto-industrial architecture includes water wheels, windmills, both vertical and horizontal, and dovecots, those vital fertilizer plants. Being "contemptuous of ideas but amorous of devices," we may find the mechanics rather than the esthetics of this architecture more to our liking.

We learn that many audacious "primitive" solutions anticipate our cumbersome technology; that many a feature invented in recent years is old hat in vernacular architecture—prefabrication, standardization of building components, flexible and movable structures, and, more especially, floor-heating, air-conditioning, light control, even elevators. We may also compare the amenities of our houses with the unadvertised comfort of, say, some African domestic architecture

5

Skeleton structure, modular building components, open plan, sliding walls, etc., have been in the repertory of vernacular Japanese architecture for centuries. Detail from an eighteenth century book illustration.

that provides a respectable man with six detached dwellings for his six wives. Or we may find that long before modern architects envisioned subterranean towns under the optimistic assumption that they may protect us from the dangers of future warfare, such towns existed, and still exist, on more than one continent.

There is a good deal of irony in the fact that to stave off physical and mental deterioration the urban dweller periodically escapes his splendidly appointed lair to seek bliss in what he thinks are primitive surroundings: a cabin, a tent, or, if he is less hidebound, a fishing village or hill town abroad. Despite his mania for mechanical comfort, his chances for finding relaxation hinge on its very absence. By dint of logic, life in old-world communities is singularly privileged. Instead of several hours of daily travel, only a flight of steps may separate a man's workshop or study from his living quarters. Since he himself helped to shape and preserve his environment, he never seems to tire of it. Besides, he is largely indifferent to "improvements." Just as a child's toys are no substitute for human affection, to him no technical contrivance makes amends for the lack of viability.

Not only is the need for confining the growth of a community well understood by the anonymous builders, it is matched by their understanding of the *limits* of architecture itself. They rarely subordinate the general welfare to the pursuit of profit and progress. In this respect, they share the beliefs of the professional philosopher. To quote Huizinga, "the expectation that every new discovery or refinement of existing means must contain the promise of higher values or greater happiness is an extremely naive thought. . . . It is not in the least paradoxical to say that a culture may founder on real and tangible progress."

The present exhibition is a preview of a book on the subject, the vehicle of the idea that the philosophy and know-how of the anonymous builders presents the largest untapped source of architectural inspiration for industrial man. The wisdom to be derived goes beyond economic and esthetic considerations, for it touches the far tougher and increasingly troublesome problem of how to live and let live, how to keep peace with one's neighbors, both in the parochial and universal sense.

6   From *Nihon Chiri Fuzuoku,* 1936.

The old photograph of an ancient cemetery on Okinawa, reproduced from a poorly printed book, is a typical example of the sort of illustration that cannot be substituted by a good recent picture. As a rule, the architectural object has suffered from decay, defacement, restoration, or has disappeared altogether. Even if it were still intact, no institution, no Maecenas, would want to underwrite the cost of visiting a work of architecture that has not already gained status in art history by having been abundantly documented in the past. Our point is that this picture, despite its technical defects, reveals a rare, not to say rarified, architectural landscape, devoid of such prosaic elements as houses and streets.

A note on the illustrations

A study project such as the one that yielded the picture material for this exhibition is inevitably beset with uncommon difficulties. With the exception of the archives of European anthropological institutes, no pertinent sources exist. Many illustrations were obtained by chance, or sheer curiosity, applied to the subject and sustained over forty odd years. Methodical travel and long years of residence in countries that afforded a study of vernacular architecture have provided the mainstays of the exhibition.

Some of the illustrations are not up to professional standards; most of them are the work of inspired amateurs or were culled from the pages of obscure publications. (See opposite page.) Moreover, with current restrictions on the movements of the citizen, it would be impossible today to procure such rare documents as the photographs of villages in the Caucasus taken in 1929 by an American glaciologist, or to duplicate the aerial views of Chinese underground communities obtained by a German pilot in the early 30s, both of whom were surprised to find their handiwork greatly appreciated at this late date.

B. R.

The amphitheaters of Muyu-uray

Anonymous architecture of a monumental kind, unknown to layman and scholar alike, can be found right on the American continent. In Peru, halfway between Cuzco and Machu Picchu, lies an ancient theater center that has no counterpart anywhere else. Built by the Inca tribe of the Maras, it comprises four theaters in the round and one in the form of a horseshoe. As might be expected, the acoustics of all five theaters are superb.

The contours of the architecture have been eroded by the elements, the site turned to pasture and farmland. Yet the basic structure is relatively well preserved. The largest theater—probably set into a meteoric crater—accommodated as many as 60,000 people. Twelve of its terraces, each about 6 feet high and 23 feet wide, still exist. The lowest circular platform of the four theaters, which corresponds to the Greek orchestra, varies in diameter from 80 to 134 feet. Water pipes, one foot wide, carved into stone monoliths, carried spring water from a nearby mountain peak.

Although nothing is known about the kind of spectacles performed, we may assume that athletic exhibitions—boxing, jumping, racing, and animal baiting—outweighed true theatricals. Peruvian archaeologists believe that the "undescribable beauty" of the landscape (about 12,000 feet above sea level) was an inspirational factor in the grandiose enterprise. As yet, the site has not suffered the ravages of tourism.

8

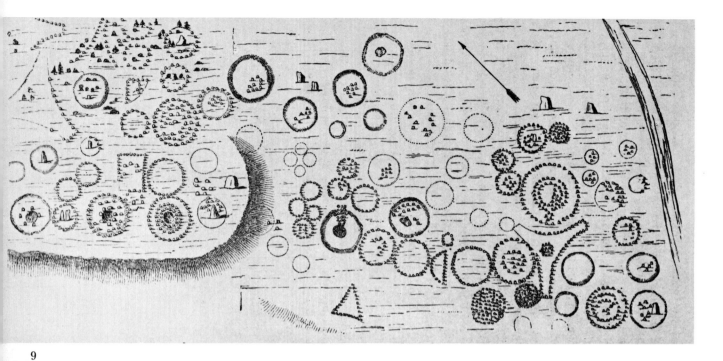

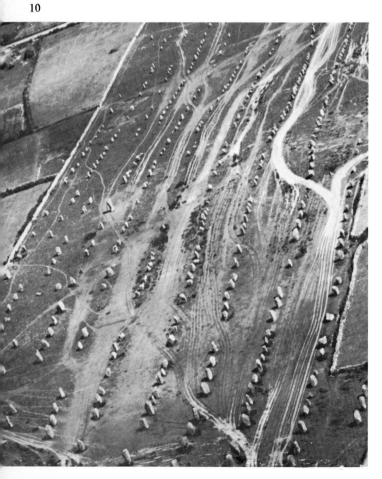

Houses for the dead

Great builders draw no line between sculpture and architecture. With them, sculpture is not "commissioned" as an afterthought or budgetary dole. Neither is so-called landscaping. The three are inseparable.

The geometric figures formed by stone slabs mark the battlefield of Bråvalla in Sweden. For all we know, the battle may never have taken place, but, since history does not concern us here, we are free to admire the design of this war memorial. It is no doubt more sophisticated than, say, the designs for the four hundred bronze and marble monuments of Gettysburg battlefield.

A partial view of "alignments" in the Morbihan community near Carnac in Brittany. The neighborhood contains a great number of prehistoric stone monuments: tumuli, dolmen, and 2500 menhirs (columns).

The aerial view of cemeteries near Lanchow, in the Chinese province of Kansu, brings to mind Isamu Noguchi's models for his "contoured playgrounds," a sculptor's rather than an architect's idea of how to improve on the surface of the land. As in other civilizations (see next pages), the houses of the dead were constructed far more solidly than those for the living.

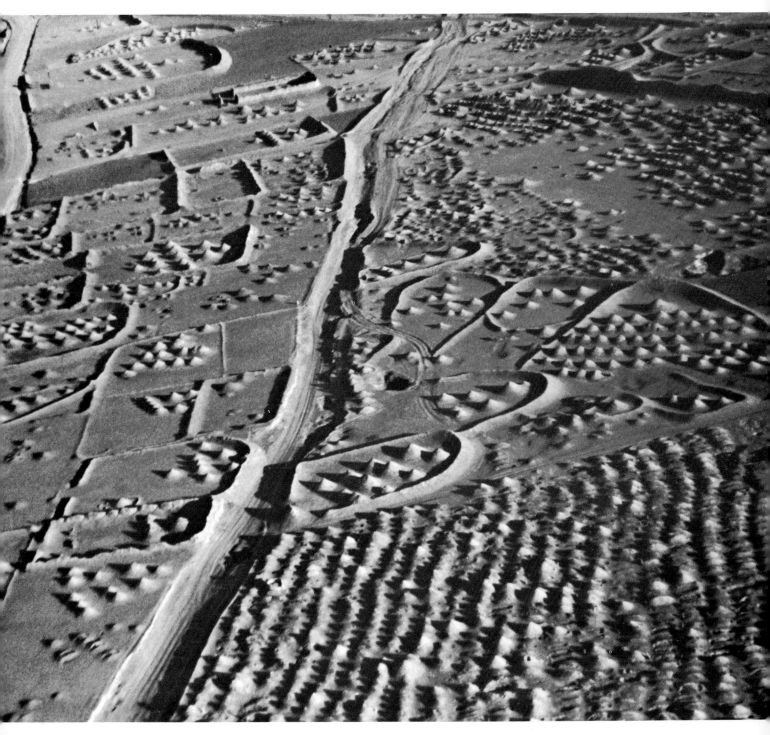

Ordek's necropolis

Looking like the model of a prize-winning entry in a sculptors' competition, this splintery architecture turns out to be indeed a great monument. No more than a ruin, the forest of wild poplar posts nevertheless forms a striking composition whose original design has been greatly improved by the corrosive action of wind-carried sand. The hill, allegedly harboring countless coffins and treasures of gold and silver, was discovered in Sinkiang some thirty years ago by one of Sven Hedin's Turkish servants, Ordek, who liked to do some private prospecting on the side.

The troglodytic town of Pantalica

Durability and versatility are characteristic of vernacular architecture. The rude chambers whose doors can be made out in the picture were cut into the nearly perpendicular declivities of the Anapo Valley by the *Siculi,* who inhabited Sicily about 3000 years ago. Originally serving as burial grounds for an adjacent prehistoric town, they were converted into dwellings during the Middle Ages. As a rule, they form multistoried apartments connected by interior passages. Similar establishments are scattered all over Sicily—near Siculiano, Caltabelotta, and Raffadale; west of Mount Etna at Bronte and Maletto; between Siracusa and the Cape S. Croce; above all, in the valley of Ispica, near Modica.

Troglodytism

Troglodytism does not necessarily imply a low cultural level. The picture of the caveman dragging his mate by her hair is a cartoonist's cliché, betraying nostalgia for bygone days, rather than a portrait of the kind of people who prefer to live below ground. Besides, troglodytic amenities vary as much as those of more conventional habitations.

The irregular holes in the oasis of Siwa, Egypt are entrances to a burial ground that has been converted into living quarters. Compared to them, the cave-dwellings on the opposite page are highly sophisticated architecture.

Opposite, a partial view of an underground village near Loyang in northern China. It takes a second glance to notice that what looks like flat roofs is earth, bare except for a few trees. Every room has a vaulted ceiling carved into the soil while the roof comes free.

Dwellings below, fields upstairs

One of the most radical solutions in the field of shelter is represented by the underground towns and villages in the Chinese loess belt. Loess is silt, transported and deposited by the wind. Because of its great softness and high porosity (45 per cent), it can be easily carved. In places, roads have been cut as much as 40 feet deep into the original level by the action of wheels. In the provinces of Honnan, Shansi, Shensi, and Kansu about ten million people live in dwellings hollowed out from loess.

The photographs show settlements of the most rigorous, not to say abstract, design near Tungkwan (Honnan). The dark squares in the flat landscape are pits an eighth of an acre in area, or about the size of a tennis court. Their vertical sides are 25 to 30 feet high. L-shaped staircases lead to the apartments below whose rooms are about 30 feet deep and 15 feet wide, and measure about 15 feet to the top of the vaulted ceiling. They are lighted and aired by openings that give onto the courtyard. "One may see smoke curling up from

the fields," writes George B. Cressey in his *Land of the 500 million: A Geography of China,*
even though there is no house in sight; "such land does double duty, with dwellings below
and fields upstairs." The dwellings are clean and free of vermin, warm in winter and cool
in summer. Not only habitations but factories, schools, hotels, and government offices are
built entirely underground.

18

19

Nature as architect

Our tendency to look at stalactite caves with cathedrals in mind, or to see castles in eroded rocks, betrays neither exceptional imagination nor artistic insight. *Ciudad Encantada,* the Enchanted City, about 120 miles east of Madrid, is a formation of cretaceous deposits covering 500 acres. The fantastic shapes, boldly cantilevered, are an astonishing sight and need no fanciful comparisons with architecture to be appreciated.

20

The baobab tree of tropical Africa, *Adansonia digitata,* sometimes reaches a diameter of 30 feet. Its wood being soft, live trees are often hollowed out and used as dwellings.

Architecture by subtraction

Occasionally, men have carved entire towns out of live rock *above ground*. The ramparts, castle, and houses of Les Baux-en-Provence were cut to a great extent from the calcareous mountain on which they stand. An important place in the Middle Ages, it has long been abandoned; the number of its inhabitants has dwindled to 250. Below, the ruin of a free-standing house.

Opposite, a close-up of one of the Göreme cones (see 48), sculpted by nature. They range from the size of a tent to that of a minor skyscraper with as many as sixteen floors. Plans of the apartment inhabited by Simeon the Stylite (in the fifth century A.D.) are shown at right. The lowest floor contained his oratory. Above it were his living quarters with a fireplace and furniture made from stone.

22

23

METER
0 1 2 3 4 5 6 7 8 9 10

24

Architecture by subtraction, continued

These churches from three continents are not "buildings" in the strict sense of the word; they, too, are carved out of rock. Below, a view of the ninth-century monolithic church of Saint-Emilion (Gironde). At right, top, a church façade from about the same time at Göreme (Anatolia). At right, bottom, St. George's Church at Lalibela (Abyssinia), carved from the rock like a sculpture and hollowed out.

26

27

From Semiramis' Hanging Gardens to the latest dam building projects, agriculture has been competing with architecture in shaping the surface of the land. Building his first wall —probably for retaining water or earth—man created space on the human scale. Piling stone onto stone was a formidable advance over carving rock. Above, terraces in the loess area in Honnan (China). Below, protective walls in a vineyard in the Canary Islands.

Below, terraced mountain top, China.

The choice of site

Man's physical freedom manifests itself no doubt in his ability to choose the place on earth where he wants to live. Whereas immature reflection tends to judge by usefulness alone, a discriminating mind may ask its share of beauty. Neither privations nor danger will deter man from selecting a spot that provides him with the exhilaration generated by a superb landscape.

Phira, the capital of the small Greek archipelago of *Thera,* is a sort of box seat in the theater of creation. It towers 660 feet above its small port on the brink of an ancient volcanic crater, and no better example could be found to illustrate the original meaning of the words uptown and downtown. Periodically devastated by earthquakes, the island has never been abandoned.

Architectural eyries

Before being introduced to the prosaic tasks of their chosen profession, students of architecture are sometimes given problems that call for tackling sites like these. It is the one and only chance in their careers for tasting the exhilaration that comes from working, if only on paper, in connivance with nature at its most magnanimous.

Opposite, one of a group of hermitic strongholds called *Meteora,* near Trikkala in northern Greece, that have been inhabited for the past eight hundred years. Access was once gained by being hoisted in a basket—the prototype of our elevators. Above, the *Peñón de Alhucemas,* one of a group of three small islands that guard the Moroccan coast southeast of Ceuta. With its turrets and batteries, the place is a sort of stationary battleship. Below: In the Spanish province of Castellón, facing the Mediterranean, lies *Peñíscola* of similar shape. A narrow sandbank joins it precariously to the mainland.

Italian hill towns

The very thought that modern man could live in anachronistic communities like these would seem absurd were it not that they are increasingly becoming refuges for city dwellers. People who have not yet been reduced to appendages to automobiles find in them a fountain of youth.

Positano (at right) changed within a few years from a simple fishing town—it was an important harbor some five hundred years ago—to a luxurious resort, without destroying the local architecture. Opposite: Anticoli Corrado, in the Sabine Mountains near Rome.

Model hill town

Mojacar, in the province of Almería, used to be one of the more spectacular Spanish hill towns until last year when tourism caught up with it. The houses shown in the photographs were torn down, or are being torn down, to make space for parking lots, hotels, apartment houses, and villas designed in bogus vernacular.

Below, a panoramic view of Mojacar. The Mediterranean Sea is visible in the upper right corner. Opposite, a close-up of the town.

39

Cliff dwellers of the Dogon

Among Sudanese tribes, one of the best known—for their art rather than for their architecture—are the Dogons. Numbering about a quarter of a million people, they live along the plateau of Bandiagara, south of Tombouctou. The photographs show one of a string of villages built on rocks fallen from high cliffs. What at first glance appears to be mere debris (below), is a mixture of flat-roofed dwellings and straw-hatted houses.

The absence of any large buildings, vehicles, or even streets, would suggest to us barbarian conditions had not extensive ethnographic investigations disclosed a highly sophisticated culture. The Dogons' architecture expresses communal organization; their religiously inspired sculpture ranks among the best of African art. Typical subjects are human figures sculpted from tree trunks that form an integral part of architecture. (See plate 156.)

Aquatic architecture

The proximity of a body of water, whether a river, a lake, or the sea, has always been of great consideration in the choice of a community. In the Orient, millions of people live much like waterfowl, more or less permanently *on* the water. Below, a sampling of houseboats in Shanghai's Soochow Creek near its junction with the Whangpoo River. The advantages of the site are evident—the waterways never need be torn up for costly repairs, drains suffer no stoppage, a bath is ready at all hours. Besides, the expanse of water functions as a cooling plant during the hot season.

To judge from the engraving above, pre-Columbian Mexico City looked much like a smaller version of Venice. Houses faced the waterfront, alleys were narrow although the central plaza seems ample. The town and lake disappeared without a trace, and so might have Venice had the canals and lagoon been allowed to fill in. Instead, Venetians stubbornly preserved their natural defenses and thus were spared the invasions of foreign armies during a thousand years.

Nomadic architecture

Tents and pavilions, "the magnificent structures that have been the pride of the monarchs of Western Asia for thousands of years, fabrications huge in size, very costly, and even if not permanent, often of extraordinary beauty," have never been seriously considered architecture by art historians, complains historian Arthur Upham Pope. The Chinese painting below more than hints at the satisfactory combination of austerity and pomp. The geometric screens of silk, set at right angles, lend grandeur to the barren camping site.

Above and opposite bottom, a holiday encampment on the Ajdir Plateau in the Middle Atlas. The tents are made from black goats' wool.

45

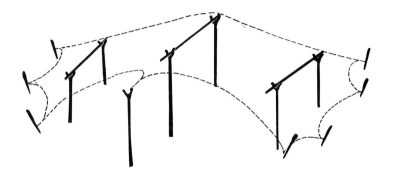

The diagram of a tent structure
(right) is from J. Chapelle,
Nomades noirs du Sahara.

Primeval forms

This is neither a case of nature imitating conical houses, nor of man copying conical rocks. The volcanic formations in the Anatolian valley of Göreme (above) were eroded by wind and water. Whether the stylized shapes suggested houses or not, the many crevices, holes, and hollows that occur in the soft stone had only to be enlarged and smoothed in order to provide habitable space. The site appealed to people with a desire for seclusion and, during the seventh century A.D., as many as 30,000 anchorites, male and female, lived here in a monastic community. Access to the thousands of chambers, churches, and chapels was, and often still is, by rope ladder.

Peasant houses, called *trulli* (below), dot the almond and olive groves of southern Apulia. They are built of annular layers of stone that terminate in a false conic cupola crowned by a keystone. The archaic house form of an early megalithic civilization, they are related to the Balearic *talyots,* Sardinian *nuraghi,* and the *sesi* of Pantelleria. Despite the passage of a dozen nations, the type has survived almost without change since the second millennium B.C. It still serves the inhabitants well.

This Göreme super-fortress shaped by nature's forces, menacing as it looks, is but a dove-cot. The entire bastion is white—the steps (at the extreme left of the picture) look like footprints in the snow—while the man-made openings for the pigeons are painted red and orange.

Architectural mimicry

Two examples of architecture where man's handiwork blends into the natural setting, thereby achieving a synthesis of the vernacular and organic forms. Below, rooftops with highly sculptural chimneys, typical of the Aegean islands. Opposite, the corner of a castle at Sotalba in the province of Avila, at the foot of the Sierra de Peñalgüete.

51

Town structures

Two different communal structures are represented by the almost pointillistic pattern of Zanzibar (left) and the relaxed geometric one of Marrakesh. A good part of the town of Zanzibar has preserved its village character with its detached huts. Streets, or whatever the vacant spaces may be called, run erratically, like raindrops on a windowpane.

Marrakesh (Morocco) is the archetype of an Islamic town with its quadrangular houses organized around interior courts. There are no traffic arteries to speak of; the cool narrow alleys of broken course often lead to dead ends.

Unit architecture

The use of a single building type does not necessarily produce monotony. Irregularity of terrain and deviations from standard measurements result in small variations which strike a perfect balance between unity and diversity. At right and below, the Spanish towns of Mijas and Villa Hermosa; opposite, the Italian Pisticci.

56

The classical vernacular

Rugged nature seems to stimulate man's artistic powers. This remarkable town, whose inhabitants come nearest to living on a volcano, is a case in point. Apanomeria is built on the brink of a crater, the leftovers of a volcano that blew up in prehistoric time. The houses, blindingly white against the masses of dark-colored rocks, represent a sort of endless sculpture.

In the 1920s, when this photograph was taken, commercial architecture was already on the march (see upper right corner). The old houses in the foreground, however, are modeled according to local tradition, their forms being no more accidental than the voices of a fugue. All of them are variations of a single dwelling type, the vaulted cell. They contain no interior staircases, each room being accessible from the outside only. The small windows prove perfectly adequate since walls and ceiling—and often also the floor—are whitewashed and thus reflect the light. No outsize buildings disturb the general harmony; even the many churches and chapels submit to the vernacular.

Fortified places

It is a curious comment on our architecture, not to say civilization, that grown-up people have been known to be in raptures over the esthetic adventures afforded by a "split level" house. Which suggests that we seem never quite able to leave the ground on our modest flights of architectural fancy. Never having a chance to wend our way through imaginatively devised space, we are unlikely to be good judges of the architecture shown here. Yet even the poor snapshots hint at some of its delights. The fascination of labyrinths and secret chambers, of murky passages and vertiginous flights of steps—all the eternal mysteries of enclosed space—is here conveyed without loss of impact by being translated into an architectural idiom that is at once complex and crystal clear. Neither house nor town but a synthesis of both, this architecture was conceived by people who build according to their own inner light and untutored imagination. Above and opposite, desert fortresses in Southern Morocco.

Family-size fortifications

Only a few hundred years ago, the skylines of many European and Asian towns bristled with slender prismatic towers, for it was both more dignified and more esthetic to fight intramural battles from the vantage point of an appropriate architecture rather than from rooftops or in streets, as is the custom in our day.

Opposite, two of the original two hundred towers of Bologna. The *Torre Asinelli* (left), 323 feet high, dates from 1109. The unfinished *Torre Garisenda* (right), built one year later, leans more than eight feet.

62

Above, a view of Vatheia, one of several fortified villages in the Peloponnesus.

Below, a Yemenite town of similar silhouette.

63

The fortified villages of Svanetia

Like Vatheia on the preceding page, these villages in Svanetia, a high-lying valley in the western Caucasus, are protected by towers. Until recently, each family had to defray its own defense budget, for as late as the latter half of the nineteenth century blood feuds and vendettas raged unchecked. "The little fortifications in which each family lives," comments William O. Field, an American glaciologist who visited the valley in the 1920s, "date from some time previous to the twelfth century. The outward aspect of the country has changed little, and the towers and castles remain dotted about the landscape, sometimes singly, sometimes in clusters of fifty or sixty."

64

67

Arcades

Neither the word *arcade* nor its many synonyms translate satisfactorily into the American language, perhaps because we have no arcades. (The penny arcade is not a variant to be considered here.) Arcades are altruism turned architecture—private property given to an entire community.

Above, arcades in Switzerland's capital, Bern, dating from the sixteenth century.

Below, a street in Aibar, in the Spanish province of Navarra. The town has preserved its medieval aspect; some streets are lined with arcades of wood or stone and many houses still have Gothic portals.

68

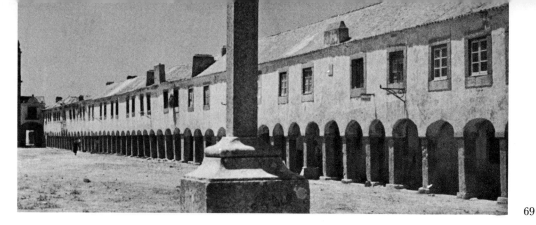

69

Above, an arcade running along a hospice at Cape Espichel in Portugal. Below, arcades around a square at Monpazier (Dordogne).

70

Arcades, continued

The disappearance of age-old pleasures and privileges is the first unmistakable sign of progress. Whereas less than a century ago every Spanish town and village boasted miles of covered ways along its streets, today they are disappearing fast.

Above, two sides of the town square of Garrovillas in western Spain. Opposite, below, a close-up of the street juncture seen in the picture above, right. It illustrates how simple design freely employed produces intricate, above all, attractive space.

Below, a street in Caldas de Reyes in Spain where the arcades have reduced the street itself to a narrow passage.

Arcades, continued

The old Moravian town of Telč in what is today Czechoslovakia consists mainly of two monumental blocks of patrician houses bordering the town square on one side and lakes on the other. Thus each house has an urban and a pastoral part, the latter ending in a garden. The town square (which is anything but square) forms the only thoroughfare. The entire length of its perimeter is covered by arcades.

Above and below, the rows of houses with their arcaded gable-ends. Opposite, an interior view of one arcade, a rural-type Rue Rivoli.

N

Covered streets

The three chiaroscuro pictures may strike terror into the heart of the urbanite because he automatically associates them with unspeakable crimes. In underdeveloped countries, however, such streets are usually as safe as a church at high mass. Still, although they are taken for granted by the natives, to us they seem unreal, devoid as they are of sidewalks, traffic lights, parked cars, and batteries of garbage cans, all of which we have come to accept as the attributes of higher civilization.

79

80 On this page, top, a street in Benabarre, Spain and, bottom, in Gubbio, Italy. Opposite, a street at the oasis Kharga, in the Libyan Desert.

Photographs can only hint at the actual experience of traversing passages through complicated space that plays on all senses: sheafs of light piercing darkness; waves of coolness and warmth; the echo of one's own footsteps; the odor of sun-baked stones. The sum of these impressions adds up to an esthetic adventure that, modest though it is, we are usually denied.

82

83

Semicovered streets

Less sturdy than arcades but gayer and more airy are the lacy coverings that are the delight of oriental streets and courtyards. Their shadow-plays are staged with simple means: canopies of trellises, mats, nets, or vines are turned to good account for distilling the raw sunlight into a sort of optical liqueur.

All examples are from Africa, except the last of the small pictures, which shows *toldos,* canvas awnings spread across a street in Sevilla.

84

85

86

Loggie

The loggia, an old fixture of vernacular architecture, runs the entire gamut from covered walkways through more or less protected balconies and galleries to columned halls.

Opposite, a wing of the Greek monastery Simon Petra on Mount Athos. Above, a panoramic view of Aul Shreck in the Caucasus. Below, houses on the main square of Chinchon near Madrid, whose loggie serve as theater boxes on the occasion of bullfights.

Quasi-sacral architecture

Among some of the least known manifestations of rural architecture are the granaries in the Spanish province of Galicia, the northwest corner of the Iberian peninsula. The inhabitants of that region descend from the Celts who invaded the continent around 500 B.C. Their rude, circular stone huts can still be found in mountain districts, yet it is the *horreos*, the corn cribs, that most deserve our attention. Built for eternity, resembling nothing so much as chapels *à pilotis*, they are conspicuous for their severe lines. Such dignity is by no means accidental—most peasants have a religious respect for bread and the stuff that goes into its making.

Put together from large granite slabs, a horreo is fire- and vermin-proof. It rests on pillars topped by circular stones that act as rat-guards, and, incidentally, are the forerunners of the classical capital. Interstices in the walls serve for ventilation. Folklore has it that horreos go on walks at night.

Granaries, continued

Cultural ties between northern Portugal and the rest of the country have never been as strong as with the neighboring Spanish province of Galicia. Not surprisingly, horreos (see preceding pages) have their perfect counterpart in the Portuguese *espigueiros*. In the rural community of Lindoso, where harvesting is a collective task, these granaries are the dominant feature. They have been placed in a privileged position to take advantage of the winds (for ventilation) and to facilitate transferring the grain to the castle in case of invasion.

Below: A view of the granaries from the castle. The land on which they stand consists of natural granite terraces that serve as threshing floors.

93

94

Small-capacity granaries

The miniature silos are from Yenegandougou (above), Korhogo (at right), and Diebougou (far right), on the upper reaches of the Volta River (Ivory Coast), about 400 miles from the sea. The fourth picture (opposite page, top) shows a Sudanese type.

While the leggy substructures of the Iberian stone granaries may have given rise to the popular belief in their nightly escapades, the potbellied type among these African storehouses suggests nothing so much as a propensity for dancing. Their anthropomorphic character is underscored by such decorations as the human face (above).

Storage towers

The granaries of the Dogon people (see 40, 41) in what was once the French Sudan are hardly less monumental than those of Galicia or Libya. Both the square towers (above) in Bandiagara, and the stalagmitic ones (opposite) near Mopti, take advantage of rocky overhangs.

Storage fortress

Whereas in Lindoso (see 93, 94) the individual granaries are located for safety's sake next to the castle, in Libya Cabao the storehouses themselves form a fortress. The steps leading to the upper floors are related, esthetically, to that singular feature of the American vernacular, the fire escape.

Fertilizer plants

In the Western world, pigeons take their place somewhere among such pests as houseflies or chiggers; whether nuisance or menace, most people look forward to their extinction. Not so in Eastern countries, where pigeonry is held in the highest esteem. The birds' droppings are collected in special towers that work on the principle of a piggy-bank. When filled, they are smashed and their precious contents put to use.

Opposite, a battery of pigeon towers at Lindjan near Isfahan.
Above and right, pigeoncots in the Nile Valley.

Engineering without engineers

Some of the contraptions of primitive technology may earn the contempt of today's engineers, yet their charm cannot be matched by modern machines. This timeless Syrian water wheel lifts water from the Orontes River into aqueducts for the houses and gardens of Hama. The wheel is 64 feet tall and does double duty as a gigantic mobile—a combination of ferris wheel and diving board—for Hama's privileged youth.

Pile dwellings

Pile dwellings held a special fascination for the founding fathers of modern architecture who adopted them as *architecture à pilotis*. Yet they have never been adopted for practical purposes.

Primitive builders, being more realistic, have long been living in the safety of their penthouses. Examples from three continents illustrate applications of elevated platforms. The simplest kind are fishing stations, such as at Vieste, Italy (opposite top), and Stanleyville, Congo (opposite bottom).

Top: The entire Chinese village of Ho Keou in Yunnan province is built on stilts, above high water level. Bottom: A tree-house in the village of Buyay, located on Mount Clarence in New Guinea.

Skeletal architecture

"Upon the mountain slopes steep by the lake, stand the rows of naked pillars rising out of the green foliage like ruins of temples: white, square pillars of masonry, standing forlorn in their colonnades and squares . . . as if they remained from some great race that once worshipped here." Characteristically, a poet, not an architect, discovered the charms of this exotic architecture. Around 1912, D. H. Lawrence lived on Lake Garda, and there wrote his essay *The Lemon Gardens*.

The *limonaie* form terraced labyrinths, enclosed by high stone walls and guarded by ferocious dogs. During the winter months, the lemon trees, some of which have been bearing fruit for 150 years, are protected from cold and snow by roofs of wooden boards, while glass panels are inserted between the 40-foot-high columns. The photographs, taken in summer, show the rustic conservatories stripped of roofs and walls.

112

111

The air-conditioners of Hyderabad Sind

These unusual roofscapes are a prominent feature of the lower Sind district in West Pakistan. From April to June, temperatures range above 120°F., lowered by an afternoon breeze to a pleasant 95°. To channel the wind into every building, "bad-gir," windscoops, are installed on the roofs, one to each room. Since the wind always blows from the same direction, the position of the windscoops is permanently fixed. In multistoried houses they reach all the way down, doubling as intramural telephones. Although the origin of this contraption is unknown, it has been in use for at least five hundred years.

113

114

115

Celestial architecture

Among abstract architecture, some of the most imposing examples stand in Jaipur, India. They are gigantic astronomical instruments built in the eighteenth century to the plans of Maharajah Sawai Jai Singh II. Their purpose was to achieve greater accuracy of astronomical data than that available from portable brass instruments. Since they never lived up to expectations, they represent that rare instance of pure, or nearly pure, architecture of a functionless kind.

116

The photographs at left and right show the "supreme instrument," Samrat Yantra, and a dozen similar, smaller structures.

At right, one of several hundred small-scale observatories in the Portuguese fishing town Olhão. They are the local equivalent of our widows' walks.

Symbolic vernacular

Only in our time are towers built for profit and usury. In the past their significance was mainly symbolic. Apart from the functional defensive towers, they usually expressed religious sentiments—faith, hope, grief, and the like. Spires, minarets, and pagodas were, or are, essential parts of buildings intended for launching prayers; only the notorious Tower of Babel spelled, unaccountably, blasphemy.

119

From left to right: The Tower of Samarra in Iraq, built eleven centuries ago. The 140-foot ascent has to be made without benefit of railings.

The thirteenth-century towering tomb of Shakh Shibab al Din 'Umar al-Suhawardi at Baghdad.

Ardmore Tower in Waterford County, Ireland.

120

121

122

123

Ungarnished castles

The founding fathers of modern architecture took more than one cue from Spanish castles. Functional, austere, and remarkably free of confectionary château-style detail, the volumes of these fortifications are composed mainly of cubic and cylindrical forms.

Above, Montealegre in the province of Valladolid. Opposite page, top, Villarejo de Salvanes, near Madrid. Bottom, a primitive type of fort in Swat State, on the North-West Frontier of west Pakistan.

125

126

Grass structures

Indigenous building methods often show great daring and elegance. The soaring framework (left) for a men's clubhouse at Maipua, in the Gulf of New Guinea, is made of bamboo poles and will be covered with thatch. (Bamboo is not a tree but a grass that may attain a height of eighty feet. For another imaginative bamboo structure see 153.)

127

At right, two working stages and the final result of a construction method used in southern Iraq. The building material is giant reed (*fragmites communis*) that grows along the lower Tigris and Euphrates, where it attains a height of twenty feet. It is bound into fasces, stuck into the ground and bent into parabolic arches. Mats woven from split reed serve for roofing. The interior is bare of furniture; carpets and a hearth for brewing coffee are the sole fixtures.

128

Wood in vernacular architecture

Log cabins are not the only architecture that one can make with unsawed tree trunks. In the two examples shown, this material achieves monumentality, tempered by elegance. Below, a row of *torii* flanking the approach to the Inari Shrine in Kyoto. A *torii* is a kind of square arch, accessory to shinto shrines; its origin is unknown.

Opposite: This interior, reminiscent of Piranesi's fantasies, consists of shorings in the eleventh-century salt mine of Wieliczka in Poland. This underground labyrinth extends over sixty miles and reaches a depth of 980 feet. The seven levels, one below the other, are connected by flights of steps.

Enclosures

Garden walls, hedges and fences are looked upon with suspicion by people who are allergic to privacy. Still, screens of every conceivable sort have always been indispensable requisites of civilized architecture. The perpendicular view of Logone-Birni (Cameroun) at left reveals such an abundance of enclosed outdoor spaces as to make the roofed-over buildings seem almost accidental.

The partial enclosures at right are windscreens in Shimane Prefecture in Western Japan. To achieve solid buffers against winter winds and snowstorms, the farmers coax pine trees into thick, L-shaped hedges about fifty feet high. In some parts of Northern Japan, straw screens of similar height are put up during the winter months around houses and, sometimes, around entire villages.

Rural architecture

The aerial view of this village of Zambian herdsmen recalls the mycological phenomenon called witches' rings, where certain mushrooms grow in perfect circles. Here, a thousand thatched huts form a circle around the chief's enclave, composed of huts for his many wives. The largest hut belongs to his favorite wife, while he lives in a foreign-style, flat-roofed wooden box. The hundred-odd pens accommodate 5000 cattle.

133

Opposite page, a segment of the ring shown at right.

134

135

136

Woven palaces

In civilizations less ponderous than ours, enclosures made from woven matting are considered fit for kings. The free-form walls (above) screen the royal court of Lealui in Zambia, the former Northern Rhodesia.

Opposite, a house in the royal quarter of Bakuba (Congo).

At right, a detail of the Palace of Justice at Aloa Bay in the Solomon Islands.

137

Movable architecture

Many so-called primitive peoples deplore our habit of moving (with all our belongings) from one house, or apartment, to another. Moreover, the thought of having to live in rooms that have been inhabited by strangers seems to them as humiliating as buying second hand old clothes for one's wardrobe. When they move, they prefer to build new houses or to take their old ones along.

138

Moving day in Guinea (above), and in Vietnam (opposite below). At left, two donkeys carrying structural elements, to be assembled into huts. Rendille nomads, Kenya.

Sometimes the borderline between clothes and habitation becomes blurred, as between a raincoat and a pup tent. Empty baskets (opposite top) may double as cover against the elements, portable roofs become umbrellas, and vice versa. Cherrapunji, India.

140

141

142

Vegetal roofs

In a genial climate, buildings often consist of little more than a roof that acts as parasol and *parapluie*. "We first spread a parasol to throw shadow on the earth," writes the Japanese novelist Tanizaki, "and in the shadow we put together a house." From the wealth of roofs made of vegetable matter, the three shown here are technically impeccable. The fluffy covering of the Kirdi hut (left) is as much a triumph of indigenous architecture as the heavy thatch roof from the Sudan (below). The roof with earflaps reaching to the ground (right) is characteristic of the vernacular of some valleys in the northern provinces of Japan. Compared to some industrial roofing materials, thatch is everlasting (not to mention its being a superb insulation against heat and cold), but good roofers are hard to come by these days. Many old Japanese farmsteads which formerly blended into their natural surroundings today advertise their presence by shiny new tin roofs.

143

144

The primeval vault

The vaulted roof is often found in the neighborhood of troglodyte dwellings, yet their exact relationship has never been properly established. The Theraen house, illustrated here, is the earliest type. The standardized dwelling unit consists of a rectangular cell with barrel vault, on which another identical unit is often superimposed. The photograph at right clearly shows the transition from cliff-face dwellings to half-dug and, eventually, to free-standing houses. Some houses have a flat roof added for drying fruit and vegetables (see also 1). Specimens of the vaulted cell-house are not confined to the Aegean Sea but are also found along the Tyrrhenian.

146

Sail vaults

We usually judge enclosed space in terms of construction cost or rental fee; its sensual effect rarely makes itself felt except perhaps in a yearning for "high ceilings," regardless of a room's proportion. But at least this hints at the important role played by the lid of every architectural container. Vaulted ceilings, especially, seem to impart a sense of comfort.

In Iran, where vaulting is almost synonymous with building, a townscape seen from above clearly discloses the inner organization of every building. At Isfahan (below), houses of God, houses of men, even streets, are covered with voluptuously undulating roofs. The row of cupolas stretching diagonally across the picture covers a bazaar street.

149

Both, the caravansarai (above) and the teahouse (below) stand in the town of Qum, near Teheran. Their walls are of stone rubble, the vaults and arches of mud brick. The nine bays of the teahouse are covered by five domical vaults and four segmented vaults, resting on four piers and the peripheral walls. The vaults of the 21-bay caravansarai, flanked by ramping segmented vaults, have 4-pier internal supports for maximum elasticity. Swelled, as it were, like a sail in the wind, this type of vault is indeed referred to as *volta a vela,* a sail vault.

150

151

Mason versus architect

"Give a mason bricks and mortar," writes Jamshid Kooros, an M.I.T.-educated Persian architect, "and tell him to cover a space and let in light, and the results are astounding. The mason, within his limitations, finds unending possibilities, there is variety and harmony; while the modern architect with all the materials and structural systems available to him produces monotony and dissonance, and that in great abundance."

Two vaults in the Masjid-e-Jameh at Isfahan. Probably fifteenth century.

Vernacular virtuosity
Truly magical effects are often achieved with modest means. At left, a Japanese arbor composed of bamboo poles and climbers. Below, the cupola of a Turkish bathhouse—a whirlpool of bright stars, arrested, as it were, in its movement. The luminous disks embedded in the dome are thick, lenselike glass blocks.
Iznic, Turkey. Othmanli period.

Caryatids, plain and polychrome

This rapid review of non-pedigreed architecture, concerned as it is mainly with its broader manifestations, cannot be expected to touch on the delights hidden under its roofs. These two pictures, therefore, merely *hint* at the intimate architectural aspects. The anthropomorphic pillars at left support the roof of the palace at Ketou (Dahomey), the one at right stands in a communal rest house of the Dogon (see 41). Less distant perhaps and less ladylike than the *Kore* of the Erechtheion, they are linked to modern Western art. Museum pieces in our eyes, they represent rather common fare in some superbly under-developed countries.

Sources of Illustrations